CHEMICAL DEPENDENCY AND THE DYSFUNCTIONAL FAMILY

Many young people feel that they have no one to help them deal with their problems with drugs and alcohol.

THE DRUG ABUSE PREVENTION LIBRARY

CHEMICAL DEPENDENCY AND THE DYSFUNCTIONAL FAMILY

Jeff Biggers

The Rosen Publishing Group, Inc.
New York

Published in 1998, 2000 by The Rosen Publishing Group, Inc.
29 East 21st Street, New York, NY 10010

Copyright © 1998, 2000 by The Rosen Publishing Group, Inc.

Revised Edition

Library of Congress Cataloging-in-Publication Data

Biggers, Jeff.
    Chemical dependency and the dysfunctional family / Jeff Biggers.
        p. cm.—(The drug abuse prevention library)
    Includes bibliographical references and index.
    Summary: Discusses the causes and dangers of chemical dependency, its effects on the family, and ways to get help in dealing with this problem.
        ISBN 0-8239-3269-9 (lib. bdg.)
    1. Drug abuse—United States—Juvenile literature. 2. Alcoholism—United States—Juvenile literature. 3. Problem families—United States—Juvenile literature. 4. Children of narcotic addicts—United States—Juvenile literature. 5. Children of alcoholics—United States—Juvenile literature. [1. Drug abuse. 2. Alcoholism.] I. Title. II. Series.
    HV5809.5.B54 1998
    362.29'13'0973—dc21   98-20873
                                                                            CIP
                                                                             AC

Manufactured in the United States of America

Contents

Introduction

"This is so typical," Shaneen Rand says, eyeing the mess as she enters the house. Her stepbrothers, ten-year-old Jesse and six-year-old Mikey, are glued to the television.

"Hey, Shaneen," Jesse says, "what's for dinner?"

"How should I know?" Shaneen answers. "Do I look like Mom?"

"No, but Mikey and I are hungry."

"Where's Mom?" Shaneen asks nervously.

"We don't know," Jesse says. "She was leaving right when we got home."

Shaneen looks at the clock. It's almost 7:30. Her stepbrothers have been home alone for more than four hours, with no dinner.

Shaneen is frustrated. If she doesn't pass her algebra test tomorrow, she could fail math. Her *grades have been slipping, but she is trying to get back on track. It's not easy, though. She doesn't get much support at home. Her mom is hardly ever around, and when she is, she's either drunk or hungover and very crabby.*

Shaneen has learned to stay out of her mom's way. Shaneen's dad, who moved out a year ago, is always busy with his new wife. Jesse and Mikey are too young to help and most of the time Shaneen finds herself having to take care of them.

Shaneen is overwhelmed by all of her responsibilities. After all, she's only fifteen. She calls her friend Jayna to talk.

"I know just what you need," Jayna says. "I'll pick you up at ten o'clock."

After Shaneen heats up some frozen pizza for her stepbrothers and then puts them to bed, she heads for the park with Jayna. Jayna pulls out some beer and hands a can to Shaneen, who pops it open, takes a big swallow, and closes her eyes to try to shut out the night sky— and the problems that come with living in her dysfunctional family.

Ray Coban hasn't left his room all weekend. On Monday afternoon, the housekeeper, Mrs. Stanley, knocks on his door.

"I'm taking Sara to a movie. Would you like to come?" she asks.

8

"No," Ray answers.

"Did you do your homework?"

"You're not my mom. Why do you care?" Ray asks angrily.

"Ray, I'm here to take care of you and Sara until your parents get back next week."

Ray feels as though his parents are never around. They're always either away on business or off on some fancy vacation. It doesn't seem fair that he and Sara have to stay home with Mrs. Stanley all the time.

When Mrs. Stanley and Sara leave, Ray feels around under his mattress until he finds what he is looking for: his stash of cocaine. He does a line and then lies back in bed.

Dysfunctional Families

Although these two families have very different problems, both are dysfunctional, meaning that the problems are so overwhelming that the families cannot function properly. Both families also involve drug or alcohol abuse, which is not at all unusual in dysfunctional families.

In fact, dysfunctional families and chemical dependency often go hand in hand. Sometimes, chemical dependency causes a family to become dysfunctional. For example, Mrs. Rand's alcoholism has contributed to problems such as divorce, neglect, and, finally, Shaneen's own alcohol abuse.

In other cases, living in a dysfunctional family leads to chemical dependency. Ray uses cocaine to deal with his feelings of anger toward his parents. In this case, the chemical dependency is not the cause of the family's dysfunction, but a result of it.

Teens and Drugs

Teen drug and alcohol use is a widespread problem. According to a 1998 study, over two million Americans between the ages of twelve and seventeen—almost 10 percent— reported having used drugs at least once.

Though most teens start taking drugs to relax or to get high, many eventually become addicted. In other words, they use drugs or alcohol because they have become chemically dependent on them. Quitting becomes very difficult because it leads to painful withdrawal symptoms, which are discussed in chapter 5.

Help Is Out There

There are many sources of help for teens who are chemically dependent because of family dysfunction. If you are dealing with these problems yourself, you are not only in good company, but you have already taken a very important first step toward recovery by opening this book.

Every teenager today faces pressure from his or her peers to use drugs or alcohol.

CHAPTER 1

Chemicals Are in Control

You may have heard the terms "drug abuse," "chemical dependency," and "drug addiction." But do you really understand what they mean?

Drug abuse is the abuse of all drugs, including alcohol. However, some people separate drugs and alcohol. These people may use the term "substance abuse" to show that they are talking about all drugs, including alcohol. No matter what you call it, drug abuse means that your drug or alcohol use causes you to act in a way that hurts yourself and others.

Both chemical dependency and drug addiction describe the point at which a person has developed a tolerance to a drug. Tolerance is when you need more and more

12 | of a drug to get the same effect (or high) that you once got from smaller amounts. Someone who is chemically dependent, or addicted to a drug, also needs to use the drug to keep from going through withdrawal. Alcoholism is the term used to describe an addiction to alcohol.

Before you can understand chemical dependency, you need to learn about chemicals and the effects drugs have on your mind and body.

Drugs and Chemical Dependency

The U.S. government organizes all illegal drugs into five categories, called schedules.

Schedule I

Schedule I includes drugs that are very addictive and have no medical use in the United States. They include heroin, a narcotic that can be injected, sniffed, or smoked; both marijuana and hashish, which are from the cannabis plant and can be smoked or eaten; and LSD, a hallucinogen that can be eaten.

Schedule II

Schedule II drugs are very addictive, but can be used for medical purposes if their use is strictly controlled by a doctor.

Schedule II drugs include opium, a narcotic that can be eaten or smoked; morphine, a narcotic that can be eaten, smoked, or injected; cocaine, which includes crack and is a stimulant that can be sniffed, smoked, or injected; amphetamines, a stimulant that can be eaten or injected; and phencyclidine, also called PCP, which is a hallucinogen that can be smoked, eaten, or injected.

Schedules III, IV, V
Schedule III, IV, and V drugs are not as addictive as Schedule I and II drugs. However, they are still dangerous. Their use should be monitored closely by a doctor. Doctors often prescribe Schedule III, IV, and V drugs as medication for coughing, vomiting, diarrhea, and weight control. They include Valium, Librium, some forms of codeine, and many others.

All drugs can be addictive, even prescription drugs. However, Schedule I and II drugs pose the most danger. Anyone taking them has a high risk of developing a severe chemical dependency.

Alcohol is not classified since it is a legal, non-prescription drug. However, it is severely addictive. Many alcohol abusers become chemically dependent on alcohol.

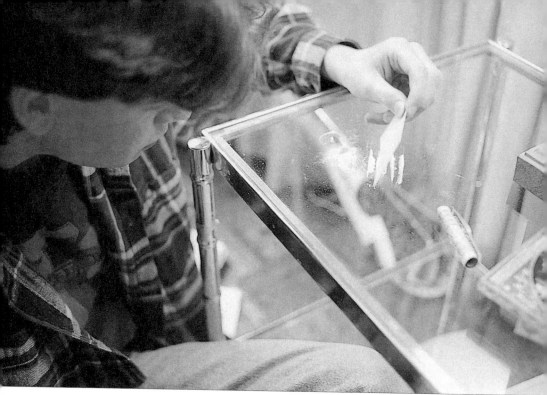

Cocaine, a Schedule II drug, is very addictive.

How Does Chemical Dependency Occur?

Most people go through similar stages that lead to chemical dependency. Not everyone has the same experiences, but these are the most common. Chemical dependency is a process. It happens at different rates depending upon the drug and the person who is taking it.

1. First, you experiment with drugs. People first take drugs for many different reasons. You may try drugs because of pressures at home, coaxing from friends, or curiosity about how a drug will make you feel.

2. Your tolerance increases. The more
   chemicals you use, the more drugs
   you need to get the same effect.

3. You may have blackouts. There may
   be times when you do not remember
   what you did when you were drinking or taking drugs.

4. You avoid talking about drugs
   or alcohol. As your addiction devel-
   ops, you try to take attention away
   from anything that will point it out.

5. You become preoccupied with drug
   use. You spend time thinking about
   drugs, plan your use carefully, and
   choose your friends based on drugs.

6. You blame others and make excuses
   for your drug use. You may even
   cause fights as an excuse to drink.
   This stage is called denial.

7. You lose control of your drug use.
   You cannot control how much you
   use or stop yourself from taking
   more drugs. You may feel weak or
   think that you do not have willpower.

16

8. Your drug use affects your family, friends, or education. Drugs may destroy your relationships. You may skip school to take drugs.

9. You may have medical, legal, or psychiatric problems. Chemical dependency brings many difficulties.

10. You lose hope. As your addiction gets worse, you may feel as though there is nothing you can do to stop it. You may feel as if your life has lost its meaning or is not worth living.

Long-Term Effects of Chemical Dependency

Chemical dependency, or drug addiction, can have very serious consequences.

Stimulants

Some drugs are called stimulants. These drugs, like cocaine and amphetamines, make you feel powerful or alert. Some people refer to them as uppers. Stimulants include cocaine, crack, amphetamines, and prescription drugs such as Benzedrine and Sanorex. Stimulants increase your blood pressure, pulse rate, and energy level. They can cause you to feel excited. They produce insomnia, paranoia, and hallucinations.

The U.S. government classifies all illegal drugs into five categories, called schedules.

Long-term consequences can include weight loss, anxiety, severe depression, violent behavior, heart failure, and suicide. Cocaine and crack also can damage the inside of the nose and cause other serious problems.

Depressants

Some drugs are called depressants. These drugs, such as alcohol and sleeping pills, can make you feel tired, indifferent, or sad. Some people call them downers. These include alcohol, barbiturates, and prescription drugs, such as tranquilizers and Valium. Depressants slow down bodily functions. Dizziness, nausea, headaches, convulsions, and memory loss can follow an initial sense of pleasure.

18

Over a long period of time, depression, fatigue, insomnia, respiratory failure, psychotic episodes (losing contact with reality completely), and suicide can occur. Alcohol also can cause blackouts, memory loss, weight gain, and cirrhosis of the liver.

Narcotics

Narcotics, also called opiates, include codeine, heroin, methadone, morphine, and prescription pain pills such as Percodan. They relieve pain. You may feel sleepy, relaxed, and extremely happy. But your pain does not go away forever. It simply is postponed. Narcotics are some of the most addictive drugs.

They can increase your risk of contracting HIV if you share needles. They can also cause heart and breathing problems, mood swings, and tremors.

Hallucinogens

Hallucinogens include marijuana and hashish, both from the cannabis plant. They make you feel relaxed. Large doses might cause agitation or excitement. Other hallucinogens, such as LSD and magic mushrooms, change your thinking and your perception of reality. You may hallucinate—see or feel things that aren't there. Hallucinogens impair judgment and coordination, putting you at risk for self-injury.

Long-term consequences, including violent behavior, paranoia, depression, and flashbacks, may occur. Marijuana also may cause low sperm count in men, infertility in women, and weight gain.

Inhalants

Inhalants are drugs such as nitrous oxide, called laughing gas. Many common products, such as hair spray, nail polish remover, glue, paint, and gasoline, produce fumes that are inhaled and can be abused. Taking inhalants may slur your speech, impair your coordination, and cause you to feel drunk. They can slow your breathing and cause nausea and vomiting.

Over a long period of time, use can lead to brain damage, severe depression, nerve damage, suffocation, and sudden death.

Chemical dependency has severe consequences for your body, brain, and relationships with other people. What starts out as a careless experiment with drugs can begin a long journey toward drug addiction. For some people, that journey ends in disease or even death. That's why it is important to get help before it is too late.

What Is a Dysfunctional Family?

Shaneen's Family

Shaneen's mother gets drunk quite often. Shaneen has had to clean up Mrs. Rand's messes more than once, and she has also found herself apologizing and making excuses for her mom's embarrassing behavior.

Shaneen has had to take on many of the responsibilities at home. She cleans up, fixes meals for her brothers, and pays the bills—all the things that her mother is supposed to be doing. Shaneen resents having this much responsibility. But she knows that if she doesn't take care of things, no one else will.

Shaneen's life at home is full of confusion, abuse, disorder, and pain. When things get to be too much for Shaneen, she escapes with a six-pack of beer.

Ray's Family

From the outside, the Coban family has always seemed perfect. Ray's parents have high-level jobs and make a lot of money. The family lives in a big house in a nice neighborhood. The problem is that Mr. and Mrs. Coban's jobs keep them away from home a lot.

Mrs. Stanley, the housekeeper, has been given most of the responsibility for raising Ray and his sister. Sara is still too young to really understand that this is not the way things are supposed to be, but Ray feels abandoned and neglected. He feels as if his parents don't even really know him. He has turned to drugs to fill the void where his parents' love and affection should be.

In a sense, Shaneen and Ray are emotional orphans. Their parents are consumed with things such as their jobs, their friends, or drugs. Neither Shaneen's nor Ray's parents have been supportive as role models, teachers, or positive influences.

Every family has problems. No family is perfect, and no one should feel bad because his or her family is going through a difficult period. The difference between occasional spats, disagreements, and even turmoil and real dysfunctional behavior is that dysfunctional behavior

22 | has more serious and long-lasting consequences. Dysfunctional families can't rebound. They cannot forgive and go on. They drift further apart. They may be on the verge of having a complete breakdown.

What Families Need

In order for a family to be functional, family members' needs must be met. All families cannot meet all these needs all of the time. This does not mean that your family is dysfunctional. However, if your family cannot fulfill many of the needs, or cannot fulfill them a majority of the time, then you may need help.

Survival

Families need to provide each other with life's basic necessities. These include food, shelter, clothing, and health care.

Safety and Security

Family members should feel safe physically and emotionally in a family. Parents have a responsibility to protect their children from abuse—physical, sexual, and emotional.

Love and Belonging

Family members need to feel loved. They should know they are welcomed and valued.

Every member of a family needs to feel secure in order to grow.

Self-Esteem
Having self-esteem means that you realize that you are an important, capable, worthwhile person. A family that values, supports, and encourages each member meets its need for self-esteem.

Growth
Everyone has to grow and change throughout his or her lifetime. A family that nurtures its members with love, respect, and open communication helps its members to grow emotionally.

Skills for Independent Living
There is a lot to learn before someone can live independently. Family members need

24 | to learn how to solve problems and to make decisions wisely.

What Is a Dysfunctional Family?

Dysfunctional means something that does not work. A dysfunctional family is a family that does not meet the needs of its members. Many things can cause a family to be dysfunctional. A dysfunctional family might not support or show love for its members. It may not provide any emotional care—it might be full of threats, insults, physical violence, and tremendous conflict. Members may neglect each other. Parents may be unable or unwilling to be part of their children's lives physically or emotionally. They may abuse each other physically, emotionally, or sexually.

In dysfunctional families, young people often are solely responsible for themselves. They may find themselves making decisions about everything from schoolwork to friends and jobs. As you get older, you must make your own decisions. But teens in dysfunctional families have not been taught how to make smart choices. Instead, they must figure things out for themselves.

These teens often do not have role models or a sense of order in their lives. Teens in dysfunctional families have to face the world on their own.

What is a dysfunctional family? How do I know if my family is functioning "normally"?

Many teens living in dysfunctional families turn to alcohol or drugs for relief. These teens use drugs or alcohol to dull their pain and to cope with their chaotic lives. They do not see any other way to escape their families, and no one in their families is around to help them. In a dysfunctional family, the other family members often are so wrapped up in their own problems that they do not notice the teen's drug abuse. The abuse gets worse and worse until the teen becomes chemically dependent.

A Scale of Dysfunction

Almost no family is entirely functional or dysfunctional, just as no person is all good or all bad. Most families fall somewhere in

26 the middle of the scale. Remember, every family has problems. Dysfunctional families usually have more problems, ones that are more complicated and harder to solve.

Obvious Dysfunction

Shaneen's family is an example of obvious dysfunction. Shaneen tries to hide her family's problems, but it's easy to see that things are not right.

Several types of dysfunction are present in Shaneen's family. Mrs. Rand is an alcoholic. She puts her need for alcohol ahead of her children's needs. She is emotionally abusing Shaneen and her stepbrothers by not providing them with the love, comfort, and discipline they need. She also yells at Shaneen and the boys fairly often because she is not feeling well enough to cope with their, as well as her own, everyday needs.

Shaneen tries hard to take care of Jesse and Mikey and to make up for all the things that their parents don't do for them, but Shaneen has her own problems to sort out. The fact that both Shaneen's father and her stepbrothers' father are not around just makes matters worse for Shaneen.

In a seriously dysfunctional family, very few of each member's needs are met. Though Shaneen's family is surviving, they are definitely not thriving. No one feels safe, there is usually not enough food or money, and Shaneen, Mikey, and Jesse feel nervous when their mom is around because conflict could occur at any time.

Shaneen and her family are in serious trouble. They struggle with dysfunction on a daily basis. Their basic needs are not met. They are struggling so hard just to survive and make it through each day in one piece that there is no room to be concerned about growth, communication, education, and skills for independent living.

Subtle Dysfunction

The problems in Ray's family are more subtle than those in Shaneen's. Ray and his sister have what they need to survive—food, clothing, shelter, safety, and security—but they don't have what they need to thrive and be happy.

Ray's parents are workaholics, which means that they put their careers before everything else, including the needs of their children. Mr. and Mrs. Coban do not actively participate in the care and upbringing of their children and take very little interest in Ray and Sara.

Ray used to work very hard at school to gain approval and love from his parents, but

A codependent teenager may cover up an addict's behavior, accidents, or neglect.

when that didn't work, Ray stopped trying. As a result, his grades have dropped. But there's really no one around to care or to talk to him about it; Ray's parents haven't been to school to speak with his teachers in years.

Ray also used to push himself extra hard to perform well in baseball games and track meets to get his parents' attention, but they never came to any of his sports events. Ray was so hurt and angry that he quit the teams. His parents never even noticed.

Mr. and Mrs. Coban never talk to Ray about things that are important to him. In fact, they rarely communicate with him at all, aside from the postcards they send on their travels.

Ray's parents are failing to teach their kids about being part of a family and are setting a poor example of nurturing. As a result, Sara and Ray may go on to repeat their parents' mistakes.

Although the dysfunction in Ray's family is harder for an outsider to spot than the dysfunction in Shaneen's family, the results are just as disastrous. Like Shaneen, Ray has turned to drugs to try to escape from his problems. Using drugs to cope with life in a dysfunctional family is discussed in more detail in chapter 4. But first, it is useful to understand the concept of codependency.

CHAPTER 3

Codependency

Shaneen, Ray, and their families are codependent. Codependency is a pattern of behavior that results in unhealthy relationships. It may mean that there is an unequal amount of give-and-take in a relationship, or that there is a lack of clear personal boundaries (limits) between two or more people.

Caring Codependents

Codependency is found in many troubled and stressful families. It occurs in all kinds of dysfunctional families, especially in families with addicted loved ones. In these families, the codependents are the people who enable loved ones to continue their addiction to drugs or alcohol. Usually spouses, siblings, parents, and children

are codependents. Other family members
and friends often are codependents, too.

These codependents have very good intentions. They are trying to cope with the chemical dependency of someone they love very much. Often it seems best to make up excuses or stories to protect the alcoholic or addict. Codependents cover the accidents and chaos left by people who are chemically dependent. They have learned that this behavior helps their day-to-day survival. Also, they often cannot deal with all the emotions that the chemical dependency or other dysfunction causes: shame, guilt, anger, fear, hatred, and others.

Poor Behavioral Patterns

At the root of codependency are patterns of behavior that create unhealthy relationships. Codependents often feel as though they need to take care of other people. In doing so, they ignore their own needs. They act as "caretakers." This means that they care for someone else by doing things that the person actually could do on his or her own. They also act as "rescuers" when they try to save someone from the results of his or her own poor behavior.

A codependent may believe that the only way he or she can be happy is by making others happy.

Many codependents have low self-esteem. They believe that they can be liked by others if they take care of them. To feel good about themselves, they have to be able to solve problems for others. However, no one can solve all of someone else's problems. When codependents fail, they feel lonely, depressed, and worthless.

Are You Codependent?

Not all codependents look alike. However, if you answer "yes" to many of the following statements, you may want to take a closer look at your behavior.

- I am afraid no one will like me;
- I try to avoid conflict as much as possible;
- Other people's happiness is more important than my own;
- When things go wrong, it's my fault;
- People do not really like me. They are just pretending;
- I never do anything right.

Codependents think they are helping someone they love. By keeping the dysfunction a secret, they believe they are making things more peaceful and easier for everyone in the family.

34 | *Hiding Addiction*

Shaneen has been her mother's codependent for years. She avoids arguing with her mother at all costs. Shaneen cleans up after her mom, takes care of the boys, and makes excuses to the bill collectors when there is not enough money. She calls in sick for her mother when Mrs. Rand is hungover and can't get out of bed to go to work. Shaneen tries hard to make things seem normal to outsiders. The effort is taking its toll, and Shaneen is sinking into depression and despair.

Often codependents like Shaneen don't see a way to get help for the alcoholic or drug addict. To them, admitting that the problem exists would be abandoning or betraying someone they love. As a consequence, they often begin to use drugs or alcohol themselves as an escape.

There are better ways to cope with a parent's drug problem. Shaneen doesn't have to be codependent, and she doesn't have to drink to dull her own pain. First, Shaneen will need to learn to take care of herself. She has to focus on her own life, not her mom's. A big part of this process is acknowledging her buried feelings. Before Shaneen can move on, she has to recognize that she is angry with her mother for drinking. Shaneen also must acknowledge that

she feels emotions such as guilt, fear, and
shame about her family.

Shaneen will have to learn to communicate, too. Making excuses and lying for her mom won't help her or the boys. In contrast, talking to someone she can trust will help her a great deal. Shaneen needs to choose someone to talk to. She is considering speaking to her uncle Mike, her science teacher, and her school guidance counselor, but she is still struggling with the idea of admitting that she needs help.

Talking to someone will not only aid Shaneen in dealing with her own problems, but also eventually enable her to confront her mom about the problems in the family.

Ignoring Addiction

Codependency in Ray's family takes a different form. By ignoring their children's emotional needs and pretending that no problems exist, Ray's parents think that they are keeping the family under control. In truth, they are creating problems that will only get worse the more they are ignored.

On occasion, Ray's mom has wondered if Ray has a problem. She chooses not to say anything, though, because to mention it would create turmoil in the family. If Ray doesn't get help, however, his drug

36 problem will only get worse. Codependents often falsely believe that by not talking about the drug or alcohol addiction, it will heal itself and go away on its own.

For the time being, Ray's family can keep up the act. But Ray is doing poorly in school, has quit both the track and baseball teams, and spends almost all his time alone in his room. He feels a tremendous amount of resentment and pain. His parents think that they are helping Ray by ignoring his problems, but in reality the bad feelings remain very close to the surface, ready to explode.

Ray's parents need to step away from their busy careers and acknowledge Ray's drug problem, as well as the feelings that have caused it. They also will have to re-establish lines of communication with Ray. This may not be easy to do, and they may have trouble doing so on their own. A drug counselor can work with Ray and his family to end the codependent relationship and help Ray overcome his drug addiction.

Both Ray's and Shaneen's families are dysfunctional as well as codependent. Both families have very serious problems that they deal with in unhealthy and sometimes harmful ways. Fortunately for Ray and Shaneen, there is help available.

CHAPTER 4

Using Drugs to Cope with Your Family

*T*eens turn to drugs for many different reasons. Some cannot deal with the dysfunction in their families. Others are the children of alcoholics or drug addicts. These teens are at an even higher risk of chemical dependency than most people. Finally, some give in to peer pressure to take drugs or drink alcohol. Many of these young people do not have role models or trusted adults they can turn to for advice.

Pressures at Home
Many teens have serious family problems. Sometimes drugs and alcohol seem to be the only way to cope with family life.

Physical Abuse
Parents, stepparents, siblings, and other family members can be abusers. Physical

abuse occurs when someone touches you in a way that causes pain or physical harm.

Emotional Abuse

Emotional abuse occurs when someone's words or actions damage your self-esteem. Emotional abusers may bully you, call you names, or purposely embarrass you.

Sexual Abuse

Sexual abuse consists of uncomfortable sexual contact or behavior. It may be as violent as rape or as seemingly nonviolent as viewing pornographic movies.

Drug Abuse

Drug abuse by a family member can result in a dysfunctional family. It can lead to everything from codependency to physical abuse to a loss of family income.

Neglect

Parents who fail to provide life's basic necessities are guilty of neglect. These needs include food, water, shelter, clothing, and health care. If a family is unable to afford these things, it is the parent's responsibility to seek help to get them.

Workaholic Parent

Today the majority of parents work outside the home. Most working parents can balance their careers and their families

Parents who place more importance on their careers than on their children or their families are called workaholics.

successfully. However, when a parent's career takes priority over his or her children or family, he or she is called a workaholic.

Depression or Other Mental Illness

Many teens struggle with mental illness such as depression and anxiety. Others do not experience full-blown mental illness, but still feel unhappy, anxious, or lonely.

Children of Alcoholics

Children of alcoholics and drug addicts are at special risk to develop chemical dependency. There is strong scientific evidence that alcoholism tends to run in families. Children of alcoholics are three to four times more likely to become alcoholics than

It can be difficult to ignore pressure to use drugs or alcohol if you do not have a family that will encourage you to say no.

children of non-alcoholics. Studies show that 13 to 25 percent of all children of alcoholics are likely to become alcoholics.

Alcoholism may run in families for several reasons. First, scientific research shows that there may be a genetic predisposition to alcoholism. Having a genetic predisposition means that you have a higher risk of becoming an alcoholic than other people because of your genes. Genes are passed from parents to children. So if your parent is an alcoholic, you may have inherited genes that make you more susceptible to alcoholism.

Also, alcoholic parents pass on their behavior to their children. Children learn to do many things by watching their parents. They might learn to paint, to wash dishes, or to drive a car. Or they might learn to cope. When a daughter sees her mother coping with problems by drinking, she may be tempted to try it herself.

Children of Drug Addicts

Chemical dependency in the children of drug addicts has not been very widely studied. Scientists do not know if a genetic link exists. However, teens whose parents are drug addicts are at a higher risk for chemical dependency. Drugs may be an accepted part of their upbringing. They may simply be presented as a part of life. To these teens, drugs are familiar. They have watched their family members use and abuse drugs. When things get tough, they may try it themselves.

Peer Pressure

Drugs and alcohol tempt all teens at some time. Most young people today either have tried some form of drug or know someone who has. Many have seen their friends, their brothers and sisters, and even their parents doing drugs or abusing alcohol.

"Everybody's Doing It"

Why do people start using drugs or alcohol? Many young people drink or take drugs to

42 | impress their friends. They may be experiencing a lot of peer pressure. Peer pressure is when your friends or your peers try to push you to do something you're not sure you want to do. Everyone feels peer pressure in his or her life. Everyone wants to fit in, be accepted, and be considered important. These feelings are normal and natural. But some people try to take advantage of other people's need for approval by convincing them to do things that are bad for them.

Peer pressure is hard to ignore, especially when you do not have a family to depend on. Sure, you know what is right and what is wrong. But you also need someone to encourage you and to support your hard choices. Many young people do not have a family that will reassure them. No one may be around to tell them that they do not need drugs or alcohol to be cool or hip.

In the end, they make their own decisions—big decisions—that they really do not want to make alone. Emotionally, socially, and physically, they call the shots by themselves. Or they give in to peer pressure and let other people call the shots.

Drugs and alcohol can be hard to resist, especially if you think that you have to take them to have friends. If your family is not there for you, saying no is even harder.

CHAPTER 5

Identifying Chemical Dependency

*A*s she rounded the corner, Shaneen noticed thick clouds of smoke coming from her house. She began to run. All she could think of were Jesse and Mikey. When she got close to the house, Shaneen found the boys huddled at the edge of the lawn. "What happened?" Shaneen asked.

"We were trying to make dinner. We were hungry," Jesse said, crying.

Shaneen felt awful. Instead of being at home with her stepbrothers, she had been drinking in the park. Shaneen panicked as she noticed a police officer approaching her.

"Are you a member of this family?" the officer asked Shaneen.

"Yeah. These are my stepbrothers."

"Where are your parents?"

Some teens turn to alcohol as a way to forget the pain and loneliness they feel. However, it relieves the pain only temporarily.

"I, um . . ." Shaneen hesitated. "I don't know," she finally admitted.

"Come with me," the officer said, taking Shaneen aside for a moment. "I want you to answer truthfully: Have you been drinking?"

Shaneen didn't know what to say. She considered telling the officer the truth and asking for help, but then again, the last thing she needed was to get her family in trouble with the police.

Shaneen had thought that she could handle her family's problems as well as her own drinking. Yet tonight she had gone out drinking on a school night when she should have been taking care of her stepbrothers, or doing homework at the very least. Shaneen knew she could stop drinking whenever she wanted—or could she? She was terrified of the answer.

Ray had failed a history test—again. But he wasn't sure if he cared about the test at all. No one cared how well he did in school, and he really was more interested in cocaine than schoolwork anyway.

He was anxious for the school day to be over so that he could go home and get high. The everyday stresses and disappointments that Ray had to face were already too much for him, and now he had to deal with another failing grade.

Ray was using cocaine every day. He used as much as he could buy. Most mornings Ray had

46 | *trouble getting out of bed. When he did make it, he needed a hit of cocaine to get moving.*

As his addiction got worse, he needed more and more cocaine just to get through the day. And he hated coming down. It left him feeling exhausted, weak, and totally out of it.

Ray and Shaneen are chemically dependent. That means that they have given up control of their life to a chemical substance—drugs or alcohol.

Do you need to have a house fire or start failing school to be chemically dependent? Not at all. Ray and Shaneen have been chemically dependent for a long time. Chemical dependency is part of a long process that began with that first hit or drink.

Two Types of Dependency

There are two types of dependency: physical and psychological. Some drugs cause both. Physical dependency means that a person's body needs the drug in order to function normally. The addict may show symptoms of withdrawal when he or she goes without the drug. He or she may shake, sweat, become irritable, and in some cases even hallucinate.

Someone who is psychologically addicted does not believe that he or she can live without the drug. The user experiences a compulsive need to take the drug. Sometimes this craving occurs because the addict wants to feel the drug's pleasurable effects. In other cases the addict is afraid of suffering unpleasant withdrawal symptoms.

When someone is physically or psychologically dependent, he or she will do almost anything to get more of the drug.

Physical Addiction

Shaneen is addicted to alcohol. She needs to drink much more now to experience the same buzz she once felt from one or two beers. In fact, Shaneen can drink a whole six-pack without feeling much at all. Her body has built up a tolerance to alcohol and its effects. Tolerance, as you know, means that the body needs more and more of a substance in order to feel the same effect that smaller amounts once caused.

Like many alcoholics, if Shaneen doesn't have a drink, she may get a headache or feel like throwing up, get shaky, and have trouble sleeping. Shaneen's body actually requires alcohol in the same way that it requires food and water to function.

Psychological Addiction

Ray, on the other hand, thinks that he needs cocaine to feel normal. Without it, he is insecure, quiet, and withdrawn. But on cocaine, Ray feels outgoing and confident.

Ray's addiction is primarily psychological. The drug controls his personality and his way of thinking and behaving. Of course, Ray's body has built up the same tolerance as Shaneen's, and he needs more and more coke to get the feeling he used to get with just a little. But even when his body is not craving cocaine, Ray's mind craves it.

Most alcoholics and drug addicts are both physically and psychologically dependent. For example, in addition to needing alcohol physically, Shaneen believes that drinking makes her popular. Ray's mind craves cocaine to feel normal, but his body really does need the cocaine now.

When a person is recovering from addiction, he or she will have to overcome both the physical and the psychological aspects of dependency. Addiction is serious, and a person who is addicted to a chemical substance can't necessarily "just quit" without feeling consequences. Chemical dependency takes over both the body and the mind, and quitting is usually a slow, tough process.

Are You Chemically Dependent?
Here are some common indicators of chemical dependency:

- You need more and more of a drug to get the same high. **49**
- You find that you're willing to do anything to get drugs, even things you know are wrong or illegal.
- You no longer take drugs for excitement, but to soothe your pain.
- You take drugs to avoid painful withdrawal symptoms.
- You often feel depressed, as if the world has nothing to offer or that you have no future.
- You cannot handle normal responsibilities, like school, work, or family duties.
- You often worry about finding money to buy more drugs or alcohol.

If some of these statements seem to accurately describe you, you might be developing a chemical dependency.

If you think you may be chemically dependent, talk to someone you trust about it. If you do not have someone you can confide in, you can call a drug abuse hotline and talk to a counselor anonymously. There are also many organizations that provide information and assistance for people battling chemical dependency. Some are listed in the back of this book.

CHAPTER 6

Finding a Way Out

Shaneen was beginning to realize that things needed to change in her family. But who could she turn to? Her mom wasn't in any shape to help and her dad was never around.

Though the fire was not really Shaneen's fault, it made her realize that she had a drinking problem. Just like her mom, Shaneen had put her desire for alcohol ahead of her responsibilities. As a result, she hadn't been home when the fire started.

Shaneen thought about the people she knew and could trust. Then she remembered Kendra Dale. Shaneen had known Kendra and her family since she was a little kid. The girls didn't hang out much anymore, but she remembered how comfortable she had always felt at Kendra's house.

Shaneen decided to visit Mr. Dale. She told
him about the fire, about her mom's drinking problem, and even about her own. Mr. Dale listened quietly. He didn't get mad or yell. He didn't even say anything bad about Shaneen or her family. Instead, Mr. Dale offered to help.

Kendra's father found an inpatient program at the local hospital where Shaneen could get treatment. Shaneen could live there until she recovered. There was even financial aid available for people with low incomes.

Shaneen wasn't sure at first. But then she thought about Jesse and Mikey and what might have happened to them if the house had burned down. Finally Shaneen decided to enter the treatment program. She wanted to help her family, and she knew that the best way to help them would be to help herself first.

Ray felt sick. As usual, he decided to stay in bed rather than face another day at school. But Mrs. Stanley had other plans for Ray.

"Get up. It's time for school!" she bellowed.

"I can't," Ray said. "I'm sick."

Mrs. Stanley left the room and returned a minute later with a thermometer. When she determined that Ray did not have a fever, she asked Ray again what was wrong with him.

"My head is pounding, my body hurts, and I feel like I'm going to die," Ray said. Suddenly

52 | *everything seemed overwhelming. Although he hated to admit it, he knew that Mrs. Stanley cared a great deal about him. Ray also knew that he had come to the end of the line in terms of what he could handle on his own.*

Ray decided to trust Mrs. Stanley. He told her about his cocaine addiction. To Ray's surprise, Mrs. Stanley didn't seem mad at all. In fact, she seemed relieved that Ray had told her. It was as if she had known all along and was waiting for Ray to tell the truth.

Mrs. Stanley told Ray that she would do whatever it took to get him into a rehabilitation program. She also promised to help Ray talk to his parents about his addiction.

The Road to Recovery

The road to recovery is a difficult one, but it does not have to be a lonely one. Millions of people, including many teens, have survived the long journey back from addiction to a healthy and happy life.

Beating an addiction can be much harder for a teen in a dysfunctional family than for people who have supportive families. You may feel as though you have nowhere to turn and no one to turn to. It may seem as if you must not only beat your chemical dependency, but solve all of your family's problems, too.

No one can do all of this, however. Problems are best resolved one at a time. First you must solve your own problem—chemical dependency. After you're better, you will be better able to help your family. Taking care of yourself is the most important thing.

Inpatient Programs

A drug addict must first find immediate safety, as Shaneen did in the inpatient program. In order to recover, Shaneen needed a place where she was physically and psychologically safe. Her unstable and chaotic home life would hurt her efforts to become sober. At the treatment center, she could get the security, support, and peace that she could not find at home.

The staff at the rehabilitation center helped Shaneen begin to face her family's problems. Shaneen also learned that some families cannot be repaired. When that happens, you must start building a support network of other people. The therapists at the program taught her how to build a support network by seeking out relatives, friends, and others who could give her support and love. When Shaneen was ready to leave, she also asked the staff for help in deciding her next step. She did not have to return home if she thought it would be bad for her.

If you want help recovering from chemical dependency, organizations that can assist you exist virtually everywhere.

Outpatient Programs

Unlike Shaneen, Ray did not feel threatened at home, just neglected. As a result, he was able to stay at home during his recovery. During the day he received counseling through an outpatient center, and returned home at night.

As part of his recovery, Ray had to face his family's problems, too. It wasn't easy, but Ray managed to get his parents and sister to join him for family counseling sessions. Therapy taught Ray's family how to communicate openly, admit problems, and work together to solve them. They learned that they all had a lot of work to do. Ray had to work on beating his drug

addiction and his parents had to learn to

communicate with Ray. And their parents had to make their children a priority in their lives. All of them needed to trust one another again. Ray's family is very damaged, but with family therapy they have started to heal.

It's Your Choice

Your chemical dependency cannot be cured by someone else. No one else can save you. No one can force you to become clean. However, when you decide that you want help, there are people and organizations willing to help you. Inpatient and outpatient groups exist virtually everywhere. Support groups such as Alcoholics Anonymous, Cocaine Anonymous, and Narcotics Anonymous probably are located close to you. Schools, hospitals, religious organizations, and communities often have their own groups to help alcoholics and drug addicts recover. Many also have teen-only groups.

Through treatment, Shaneen and Ray were able to stop using drugs and alcohol. They began to deal with their chemical dependency, the problems it caused, and the pain and suffering it brought. In their rehab programs and in support groups, they learned about and met addicts who

Finding healthy and positive ways to deal with daily stress can help you beat chemical dependency.

had recovered from their addictions. They discussed what they wanted for their future, for their personal relationships, and for themselves. They talked about how to deal with old friends and offers for drugs and alcohol. They learned to resist peer pressure. They talked about rebuilding lives filled with new activities, new friends, and new plans.

Self-Help Groups

Shaneen and Ray also joined self-help groups, which were made up of teens struggling with drugs and alcohol. The self-help groups supported and encouraged them. They reminded Shaneen and Ray that many other teens were facing the same issues that they were. The groups gave them the strength to deal with old friends and old temptations. They also helped them to examine their families' dysfunction.

Most important, Shaneen and Ray realized that they had to begin new lives. They needed to deal with pain and confusion by means other than drugs and alcohol. Shaneen and Ray needed to find healthy and positive activities that would enhance their future, not drag them back into the misery of their past addiction. They were encouraged to consider activities and hobbies that they had not tried

58 before. Ray rejoined the track team and took a part-time job after school. Shaneen started volunteering to help other teens dealing with life in dysfunctional families.

Both Ray and Shaneen began keeping journals. They write about their daily experiences and how they grew and overcame the problems caused by living in their families. There is no easy way out for Shaneen or Ray, and there never will be. Despite all of their family problems, they both have to take control of their own lives. They have to take charge of their addiction and recovery.

Ray and Shaneen have similar problems, but they are from different families with different dysfunctions. Both are learning that some families can be repaired, but others cannot. In therapy, Ray is working with his parents and sister to make their home happier and more supportive. Shaneen, in contrast, might not be able to return to her family. However, Shaneen does not have to return to her old patterns of dysfunction—drinking. She can learn more effective ways to cope with her family.

Shaneen and Ray are not responsible for repairing their families. They can take charge of only their own behavior. They have to face their chemical dependency and continue to heal themselves.

Glossary

addiction Chemical dependency.

chemical dependency To need drugs or alcohol compulsively and not be able to function without them, also called addiction.

codependency When someone ignores his or her own feelings in order to protect and care for someone else.

denial Refusal to admit the truth.

depressants Drugs, such as alcohol, that slow down your body and brain, also called downers.

downers Depressants.

drug abuse Using drugs or alcohol in a way that harms yourself and others while ignoring the hazardous consequences of your drug use.

dysfunctional Not working properly.

hallucinogens Drugs, such as marijuana, that cause hallucinations.

inhalants Drugs taken by inhaling.

inpatient treatment center A program that requires patients to live there during treatment and recovery.

60 | **narcotics** Drugs, such as heroin, that dull the senses and reduce pain.

outpatient treatment center A daytime program that allows patients to return home in the evenings after treatment.

peer pressure When people your age try to convince you to do something you do not want to do.

physical dependency When your body cannot function normally without a drug.

psychological dependency When your mind desperately craves a drug.

recovery The process of getting well.

self-help program Teaches you how to help yourself by learning to improve yourself and resolve your problems.

stimulants Drugs, such as cocaine and amphetamines, that speed up your body and brain, also called uppers.

support group A set of people with a shared experience who give one another encouragement and guidance.

tolerance When you need more of a drug to get the same effect that you once got from smaller amounts.

uppers Stimulants.

withdrawal A painful syndrome that affects a drug addict's mind or body when he or she stops using drugs.

Where to Go for Help

If you are in need of immediate assistance, you can call this hotline twenty-four hours a day, seven days a week:

Al-Anon/Alateen Family Group Headquarters, Inc.
(888) 4AL-ANON

In the United States

Alcoholics Anonymous (AA)
P.O. Box 459
Grand Central Station
New York, NY 10163
(212) 870-3400
(Also serves Canada)
Web site: http://
  www.alcoholics-
  anonymous.org

Narcotics Anonymous (NA)
World Service Office
19737 Nordhoff Place
Chatsworth, CA 91311
(818) 773-9999
E-mail: wso@aol.com

In Canada

Alcoholics Anonymous Manitoba
505-365 Hargrave Street
Winnipeg, MB R3B 2K3
(204) 942-0126

Narcotics Anonymous
U 15 558 Queenstown Road
Hamilton, ON L8K 1K2
(905) 522-0332

Online Al-Anon Information Service
http://www.links2go.com/mo
  re/www.ola-is.org

Web Sites

Welcome to My Hall Closet
http://www.caprica.com/~tut
  or/closet.htm

For Further Reading

Chiu, Christina. *Teen Guide to Staying Sober.*
    Center City, MN: Hazelden Press, 1998.
Gottleib, Eli. *The Boy Who Went Away.* New
    York: St. Martin's Press, 1996.
Jamiolkowski, Raymond. *Coping in a
    Dysfunctional Family.* Rev. ed. New York:
    Rosen Publishing Group, 1998.
Neuharth, Dan. *If You Had Controlling
    Parents.* New York: Cliff Street
    Books, 1998.
Reeds, Sharon. *Everything You Need to Know
    About Drug Abuse.* New York: Rosen
    Publishing Group, 1998.
Smith McLaughlin, Miriam, and Sandra
    Peyser Hazouri. *Addiction: The "High" That
    Brings You Down.* Springfield, NJ: Enslow
    Publishing, 1997.

Index

64

About the Author

Jeff Biggers works as a freelance writer and consultant for adult literacy programs, as well as creative writing and literacy arts programs for at-risk youth. Mr. Biggers studied at Hunter College and Columbia University in New York City. He resides in Flagstaff, Arizona.

Photo Credits

pp. 2, 10, 14, 28, 44 by Lauren Piperno; p. 17 by Christine Innamorato; p. 23 by Ira Fox; p. 25 by Kim Sonsky/Matt Baumann; p. 32 by Michael Brandt; p. 39 by Les Mills; pp. 40, 56 by Ethan Zindler; p. 54 by Pablo Maldonado.